The Klutz Book of
Inventions

John Cassidy • Brendan Boyle

KLUTZ

KLUTZ®

creates activity books and other great stuff for kids ages 3 to 103. We began our corporate life in 1977 in a garage we shared with a Chevrolet Impala. Although we've outgrown that first office, Klutz galactic headquarters remains in Palo Alto, California, and we're still staffed entirely by real human beings. For those of you who collect mission statements, here's ours:

- Create wonderful things
- Be good
- Have fun

Write Us

We would love to hear your comments regarding this or any of our books. We have many!

KLUTZ®

450 Lambert Avenue
Palo Alto, CA 94306

Book manufactured in China. 52

Distributed in the UK by
Scholastic UK Ltd
Westfield Road
Southam, Warwickshire
England CV47 0RA

Distributed in Australia by
Scholastic Australia Customer Service
PO Box 579
Gosford, NSW
Australia 2250

Distributed in Canada by
Scholastic Canada Ltd
604 King Street West
Toronto, Ontario
Canada M5V 1E1

ISBN 978-1-59174-879-3

4 1 5 8 5 7 0 8 8 8

Safety Stuff

This is not an instructional book and the inventions in it are included as concepts, not blueprints for construction. We hope you're inspired by these pages and go on to create many of your own fabulous inventions. But in the meantime, please don't try to build and use the ones in this book.

Visit Our Website

You can check out all the stuff we make, find a nearby retailer, request a catalog, sign up for a newsletter, e-mail us, or just goof off! www.klutz.com

Table of Contents

*How to think
like an inventor*

Introduction

Many years ago we at Klutz began our publishing enterprise with a how-to book on the art of juggling. We didn't start the first lesson with a description of accurate throws or good catches; we started it with a step-by-step discussion of something we felt we knew a lot more about. We called it, "The Drop."

**It's all about
The Drop.**

There's a reason for that, and it's not just because we're so lame. At Klutz — and IDEO Toy Lab — we're huge supporters of big flops and grand failures. Not so much because we enjoy the experience of a creative face-plant, but out of the belief that it's an absolutely necessary step. Potholes, dog doo, and unguarded edges are always on any path worth taking and if you're not stepping into, onto, or over any of them — then the sad truth is, you're not going anywhere.

Nobody learns how to juggle without dropping a lot of balls and nobody invents anything very cool without making a lot of hysterically wrong turns.

Which brings us to this book, which seems to be about inventions, but is actually about something more — innovation, or how to think like an inventor. If you're interested in releasing your inner nutcase (which can be often used as another word for inventor) here's a thought exercise that we think will help.

Look at any common invention that we use every-day. Start with the basics. The wheel. The fork. The modern nose hair trimmer. We guarantee that each of them was originally described as "ridiculous" and preceded by many, many failures. (The wheel looks like a no-brainer winner until you realize that there were no roads, no axles, no carts, and 6 zillion years of very successful living without one.) We don't know

**The wheel.
An early failure.**

The lightbulb is a particularly funny choice as the universal symbol of "sudden inspiration" since it took Edison years to get one to work. It is, for that reason, an excellent symbol of what the real process of invention is: a long road filled with failures, each of which steers the inventor on.

the real name of the person who invented the wheel but we're willing to guess what they called him behind his back — "Nitwit."

The fear of failure, of looking like a fool — in the eyes of other tribes or, more dangerously, in your own — is the single biggest obstacle to human progress in the history of history. If we could make one single change to human DNA, removing that fear gene would be it.

But in the meantime, we have a less surgical fix. We call it "play."

Most people will tell you that "play" and "work" are opposites. Work is serious; play is playful. Playful people are wasting time; serious people are doing productive work. But serious people are also concerned about the indignity of making mistakes, whereas fools wallow in them. And since progress is filled with mistakes, whom are you going to call when you need some progress made?

Does this mean that Bozo should run NASA labs? No. But if the chief scientist at NASA doesn't push his researchers onto the thin ice of crazy ideas, his people and his results will be warm, dry, and boring.

Dignity is the enemy of invention.

The lesson here for any inventor-to-be is play with your problem. Do not be afraid. Go for lots of ideas, ridiculous to practical, and then go back looking for winners. Celebrate your mistakes, learn from them, and if people call you absolutely, 100%, no-question-about-it nuts… you're probably getting warm.

In your frozen food section
Frozen DV Dinners

As soon as you pop open the lid to one of these tasty DV Dinners and then settle back to a great movie, you'll wonder why someone didn't think of this before!

Each of these heat-and-eat gourmet dinners comes complete with a disposable, one-time-use DVD player built into the lid. Lift it up and the preinstalled movie starts automatically. It's dinner and a show! Right in your own home!

Choose from our extensive meal+movie collection, including: *Jaws* with fish and chips, *The Godfather* with lasagne, and *Babe* with pork chops.

Watch, eat, and toss.

A funner plunger

The PogoPlunger

Who says clearing out a stopped-up toilet has to be a chore? With this idea, you'll look forward to every backup. Great for kids, adults, the whole family. Let everyone experience the joy of sewage with the PogoPlunger, the perfect marriage of plumbing and jumping.

Adds challenge

Unicycle Built for Two

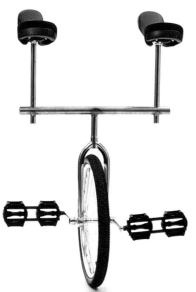

Just because you're on a unicycle, doesn't mean you can't have friends. Or at least friend.

The unicycle built for two is a souped-up model designed to double the challenge for people who find the old style just a little too easy.

Gives your pet a chance to contribute
The Wiener Cleaner

Dogs are like everybody else. They want to belong; they want to be a part of the family. But so often those feelings are frustrated by their sense of "differentness."

If your dog is troubled in this way, the Wiener Cleaner is just what the vet ordered. When chore time rolls around, and the family is all there pulling together, strap a Wiener Cleaner on your little fellow, give him a chance to join the family, and watch his spirits soar.

Don't you hate it when people borrow your stuff?

Password-Protected Stapler

How many times have you come back to your desk and discovered a staple missing from your stapler? *And it's been moved, too.* Makes you spittin' mad, doesn't it? So then you put your name on the thing, in big block letters with the words "Property of" in front. And does that help?

We didn't think so. Fortunately, you've come to the right page. With our password-protected security stapler, you can rest easy, knowing your valued office supply is safe from thieving co-workers.

If you forget your password, go online, find the site that retrieves passwords, and look up yours.

*Say "good-bye"
to umbrella elbow*

Heliumbrella

We all know the problem. It's pouring rain, you're in the parking lot, your hands are full, and the bottoms of your bags are soaking wet. Stuff's falling out everywhere.

Or maybe it's monsoon season, it's been raining for weeks, and your umbrella elbow is killing you.

At times like this, how would you like some shelter from the storm that doesn't weigh a thing? Literally?

Meet our inflated Mylar Heliumbrella. It's doorman-sized, it's completely weatherproof, and best of all, it's lighter than air. Just slide the straps under your arms and the Heliumbrella floats above your head. Hands-free.

Footwear goes ballistic

ShoeTers™

Are your feet cocked and loaded? When you jump up and down, do your enemies turn and fly? Do rockets chase them screaming down the street?

ShoeTers are just like ordinary shoes except they launch rockets whenever you jump up and down. The heels are specially made pumps that squirt powerful blasts of air that shoot rockets wherever you point your toes.

For big loads
The Crewbarrow

The crewbarrow is a three-person rig designed for especially heavy loads or wheelbarrowing competitions. A built-in seat is mounted up front for a coxswain to keep the team stepping in time.

Save dishwashing time
The Multi-Mug

Your coffee klatch is coming over this morning and you're starting to stress already. All that coffee. All those coffee mugs. And worst of all, all that dishwashing afterwards.

Wait! You've forgotten your new Multi-Mugs! You're a smart shopper and an environmentally aware one, too. By using Multi-Mugs you're able to cut your dishwashing water usage by two-thirds. And thanks to the unique equal-segment design, everybody gets their own favorite beverage. The lattes can live with the low-fats and everybody's happy. No backwash. No cooties.

Solves a gnawing problem

The Puppy Pacifier

Save your slippers, spare your shoes, rescue your rugs, and protect your potholders from teething puppies with this tooth-proof boney binky.

Elevator with built-in StairMaster

The Gym-o-Vator

You know you need to get down to the gym, but who has the time? Rushing between school, home, office, and then back again. It's crazy out there! Where are you supposed to fit that workout in?

Answer? The Gym-o-Vator! The new, workout-equipped elevator car. Turn your down time ("up" time, too!) into healthful time. After you've pushed your button, instead of standing there staring at the door, climb onto the built-in StairMaster and start taking that waistline "down" a floor or two.

High-Heel Training Wheels

Every girl remembers her first time in high heels. ("Finally growing up!") But too often the special moment is spoiled by the awkward stumble and crash resulting in embarrassing fractures and ugly contusions. There's nothing worse than finishing prom night at the ER.

What to do?

Take the high risk out of high fashion with high-heel training wheels. Sturdy, safe, yet stylish.

Relax and conch out

Ocean Ears

Here's the all-natural sleep solution for your next airplane trip. Instead of screaming babies, try the sound of soothing waves. Ocean ears consist of two conch shells on a headband that fits snugly over both ears. Slide them on (no batteries necessary) and listen to the sound of the ocean, not the engine.

Don't even bother hiding the keys
Hide-a-Car

Car thieves aren't idiots. They weren't born yesterday. They've seen the fake rocks with the keys inside. That trick's done. It's time to throw 'em a head fake and switch it up. That's why you need to think a little bigger. Instead of hiding the keys… hide the car!

This 12-foot-long hollow fiberglass rock looks just like a real one but weighs less than 30 pounds. When you're driving around town or on the highway, it mounts on the roof upside down (hardware included). Then, when you have to park, take it down and set it over the car. Now you can do your shopping fearlessly, rock-solid confident your car will be there when you get back.

Fools muggers

Camouflage Vending Machine Outfit

Street crime can take many frightening forms: pickpockets, crooks, hoods, thugs, bullies, and bad guys of all kinds. One thing they have in common, though: None of them stick up vending machines.

And that's exactly what you'll look like — a beat-up old Coke machine — once you get into this life-sized realistic-looking canvas vending machine outfit. A boon for anyone who lives in these scary times.

Comes complete with a battery-powered reading lamp for extended nighttime use.

You'll feel better.
And so will your flies.

Catch-and-Release Flyswatter

Being a fly is no fun. Eating garbage and dog doo isn't as tasty as you'd think and your average fly would switch if he could. Add to that, most flies come from large families where the parents are emotionally absent and the little ones are left to fend for themselves at an early age. Given all that, it's no surprise that a fly's adolescence minutes are marked by long bouts of depression and paranoia.

Is there anything you can do to help?

Yes. Especially with the paranoia part. Our catch-and-release flyswatter relieves the flies in your life from at least one of their nagging issues — the possibility of instant violent death from above.

Of course, it's not just about the fly's feelings either. Imagine what you'd think if you discovered that one of the flies you just smacked was less than 5 minutes old? Or perhaps a parent itself?

The catch-and-release flyswatter works just like a regular one except for the specially designed spring-loaded trapdoor. Take your safely trapped flies outside and release them by the garbage cans. You'll feel better — and so will your flies.

Great on foggy days

Rolling Ball GPS System

The steering wheel–mounted rolling ball GPS system is a low-tech alternative to finicky, unreliable GPS units that require a PhD in electronic engineering to understand anyway. Each maze is custom-designed for your common destinations (school, work, store, etc.) and each snaps into and out of place in the center of your steering wheel.

To use, simply place the ball at "Home" when you're sitting in your driveway, and then start the car and turn the wheel to guide it through the maze. When you look up — presto! — you'll be there.

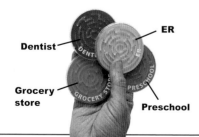

Dentist

ER

Grocery store

Preschool

Fly your kite whenever you darn well feel like it!

Windless Kite

Stop wishing and hoping for just the right wind. With this 18-foot, extendable pole—mounted kite, every day will be perfect kite-flying weather. No more frustration, no more kite-eating trees. With the windless kite, you'll be in charge of your entire kite-flying experience.

Patented rubber butt-bladders do the heavy lifting

Inflatable Booster Pants

Why are the people in front of you always so tall? Have you ever wondered about that? What are they? Zulu warriors? NBA stars? It's so reliable, it's practically eerie. Or maybe you were marked at birth. ("Please block my view. I was born to it…")

Fortunately, it doesn't matter anymore. With inflatable booster pants you can rise above them all. Here is how they work.

The next time some giant sits in front of you, just squeeze the bulb on your booster pants. The built-in pump will add air to the sturdy rubber butt-bladders and lift you up. Guaranteed up to 16 inches of additional height. Beyond that, the risk of explosion is too high and you're off warranty.

① Squeeze the…   **②** bulb to…   **③** lift you…   **④** higher.

*Takes the guesswork
out of ordering*

Scratch 'n' Sniff Menus

Introducing scratch 'n' sniff menus, the "previews" of the restaurant world. With scratch 'n' sniff menus, the mystery meat will hold no mystery. The "shoque" will be no shock. With scratch 'n' sniff menus, you'll order in confidence.

oked Pork
.............$6.95

SCRATCH

with **Spicy Salt**
.....................$5.95

SCRATCH

eed Clams with
Bean Sauce
.................$7.95

SCRATCH

ith **Bean Curd**
$4.95

SCRAT

Put your mustard where your mouth is

Squeeze-Me Silverware

Squeeze-me silverware might be the greatest advance in condiment application since the invention of the 3-foot pepper grinder. Here is how it works: Condiments (mayo, mustard, etc.) are loaded into the sturdy yet flexible plastic handle through a simple screw-on cap. On the other end is a conventional spoon or fork. As food is brought into mouth-range, a quick squeeze puts the condiment directly onto the food an instant before it crosses the tooth-line, so your condiment stays fresh and always on target.

Don't you hate it when other people use your hair-care accessories?

The Lockable Combo Comb

This is one of those inventions that we wish didn't have to exist, but the truth is there are many people out there who will borrow your brush or comb, use it, and then put it back without telling. Sometimes, depending on timing, you'll discover it's wet and that will be your clue; other times, the only evidence will be too small to see — their nasty little cooties. The result is you're left wondering and worrying every time you brush your hair.

Teeth unscrew and store in handle.

Unless you're using a combo comb! Each tooth on the combo comb unscrews and fits neatly inside the hollow handle. After every usage, simply remove the teeth, store in the handle, and lock them away with your own personal combination. Peace of mind comes to hair care.

Re-runs and reps

TV Remote Dumbbell

Forget push-ups and don't even waste your time on bench presses. If you really want that ripped look, you'll need to hit the couch and log some serious tube time.

*Never run out of
bathroom tissue again*

Reminder
Toilet Paper

Are you always running out of toilet paper at crucial moments? ("Oh, *darn!*") Are you saddened when that happens? Or is "disappointed" a better word?

Either way, here's a foolproof invention for making sure it never happens again.

"Reminder" toilet paper is just like regular toilet paper except for the last 4 feet, when it gets different. *Really* different. That's when it turns into sandpaper.

You'll be amazed at the difference. And you'll be amazed at how well it stimulates your memory.

Helps develop early musical talent

Head-Mounted Drum

Everybody knows schools are cutting back on their budgets, especially in the arts, and that's why it's more important than ever for parents to step in and help youngsters develop their musical talents.

Which brings us to the head-mounted drum, a concerned parent's dream come true. Each drum is equipped with adjustable forehead straps enabling it to mount firmly to the back of the head. Thanks to its convenient location, parents will be able to keep close tabs on their child's musical progress.

Comes with extra drumsticks in case of breakage.

Can't find your glasses?
Not a problem...

Prescription Windshield

Here's a beautifully simple way to stop worrying about your glasses when you're driving the car. With a specially made prescription windshield, everything out there will be in perfect focus. For you. Which brings up the bonus! Once your car gets a customized windshield like this, you can stop worrying about anybody stealing it. Go ahead and leave the keys inside (right next to the barf bag).

Works at the ATM, too

Portable Privacy Curtain

Your pencil-hunting days are over!

Pencil Lead Nail Polish

With pencil lead nail polish, you'll be carrying ten pencils with you at all times. No more frustration while you paw through drawers and under couch cushions. And bonus! Black is the new black. You'll be fashionable and functional, right down to your fingertips.

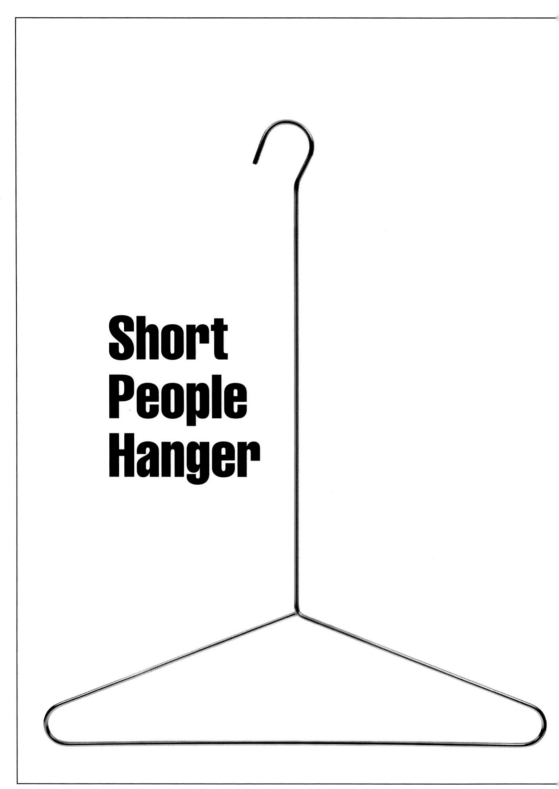

Short People Hanger

Provides the expensive fitness gym experience, without the expensive fitness gym dues

The Porta-Gym Scenic View

Sure you'd like to join a fancy fitness gym, but their fees! Who has that kind of dough?

Well, guess what? You can forget the fees. With the Porta-Gym Scenic View you can bring the gym experience directly home to you without any of the cost. Here's how. The Porta-Gym Scenic View is a framed, full-color, 8x12-inch, beautifully reproduced photograph of someone hard at work on a stationary bike. Taken from the rear.

Mount this sturdy and inspiring image on the handlebars of your own bike (all hardware included) and as you pedal around town, you'll be able to enjoy the same

Photo mounts to handlebars.

view as all the people at the fancy gyms do at no additional expense. It's the deal the gym owners don't want you to know about.

Remember: With the Porta-Gym Scenic View you can skip the dues, and still get the views.

The Never-Miss Putter

One of the chief flaws in the game of golf is the "hit and watch" problem. Players are forced to hit the ball once — and then watch powerlessly as it either goes where they want or not. This is especially problematic at the most critical moments in the game, on the greens, when the ball is approaching the cup. That's when many players say they experience the issue most acutely.

The design of the Never-Miss Putter, however, enables players to "stay in the game" throughout the entire putt. After striking the putt, if it starts to roll left or right, players may simply tweak the putter a tad and the two extendable steel rules will then gently correct the ball, allowing it to drop into the cup as originally intended.

No frozen nose

Ear and Nose Muffs

Brrrr! Winter's chill is here! Fortunately, you're warm and nose-toasty with the world's first three-point set of ear and nose muffs. Each pair is made of fuzzy warm fur-like material and designed to hit your comfort zone right on the nose.

Can't wait for
your weight?

Strap-On
Shoe Scales

We live in an age of instantaneous gratification and that's exactly the insight behind this invention. With strap-on shoe scales you'll be reading your weight to the ounce in real time. After every meal (after every bite!) you'll be right on top of it. Imagine the relief.

**Scales strap
on to any shoe.**

What you can't see, can't annoy you

Sibling Blinders

If you have a younger (or older) sibling, these blinders are designed to improve your view every time you have to ride in the backseat with him (or her). The comfortable headband means you can wear them just as well on endless road trips as well as short trips to school or the store. Life just got a whole lot better.

Lose 20 pounds by Friday

Programmable Bathroom Scale

Finally, a weight-loss device that *really* works. This programmable bathroom scale allows you to decide how much weight you want to lose and when you want to lose it. It puts YOU in charge of the whole diet process.

Let's say your goal is to lose 20 pounds by Friday evening, 4 days from now. Not a problem. Just enter the amount of weight you want to lose (in this case, 20) and how many days you'd like to do it in (in this case, 4 days). Your scale will automatically do the math and will read the appropriate weight every time you step on it between now and Friday. Guaranteed success! And you can eat like a total pig.

In our example here, the weight loss will be a steady 5 pounds a day unless you decide to override the automatic settings and go for some heroic last-day crash thing. However, most nutritionists will recommend against that since studies have shown that gradual weight loss is the healthiest and most durable.

Speaking of durable, after you've achieved your goal weight, you can lock in that number for up to 20 years, depending on your batteries. Finally, say "good-bye" to yo-yo dieting!

Lighter-than-air mail

Helium Bubble Wrap

Here's a handy way to cut your shipping and postage costs at the same time as you protect your stuff. Helium bubble wrap works just like regular bubble wrap except that the more you use, the less your box weighs.

The HeadBed

If you're a big multi-tasker (and let's face it, you wouldn't be reading this book if you weren't!), you'll appreciate the genius behind this idea. With a HeadBed on, you'll be able to attend meetings, or after-lunch classes, or just wait for the bus — and still get a nap in. It's a great way to squeeze two activities into the same time. Automatically doubles your productivity!

4TH QTR
RESULTS

You'll be itching to get back to your book…

Classic Fiction Bathroom Tissue

There's nothing quite as relaxing as sitting down to a great novel.

Well, almost nothing.

Living in today's fast-paced digital world, we know as well as you do how hard it is to find the time to absorb all the culture you're so hungry for. It's frustrating! So many symphonies… so many art museums… so little time.

But here's an idea that can help! Turn your down time into culture time with classic fiction bathroom tissue. Each roll of this squeezy-soft tissue paper is printed with the full text of a timeless classic.

Each family member gets their own novel.

You beat 'em,
you eat 'em

Chocolate Chip Checkers

Here's a chance to play checkers straight from the oven. Each of these cookie sheets is actually a checkerboard, too, with 24 ready-to-bake cookies already in place on their squares. (Twelve cookies are chocolate chocolate chip; 12 are vanilla chip.)

Just pop in the oven and 12 minutes later, you're ready to play.

By the way, any time you jump the other guy, you get to eat him.

*Frisbee for
the friendless*

The ThrowYo

Works like a boomerang, throws like a Frisbee,
and acts like a yo-yo.

The solo throw

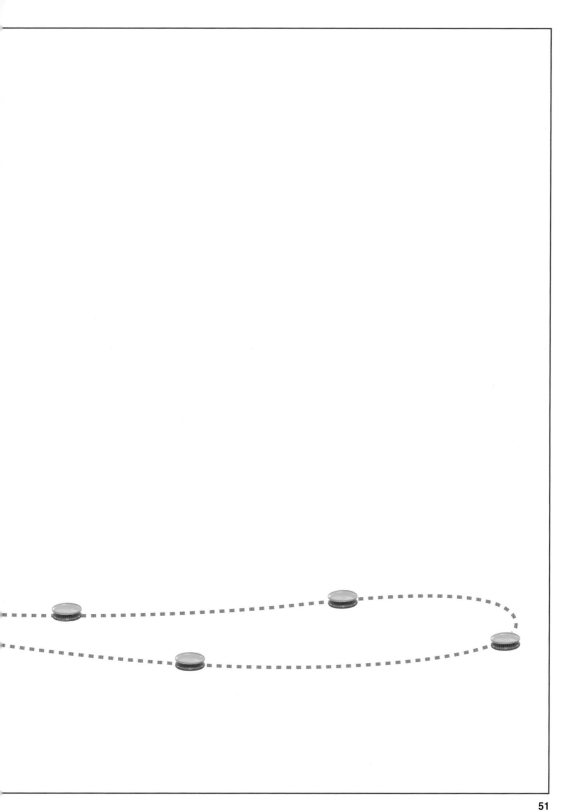

Change diapers on one side, eat dinner on the other

Diaper/ Dinner Table

Change diapers on this side.

Anyone who's ever lived in a small apartment will appreciate the efficiency built into this dual-purpose diaper/dinner table. Change the baby on Side A (in the built-in comfy diaper-changing station), then hammer the legs through to the other side and sit down on Side B to a lovely dinner.

Pound legs through to use other side.

Eat dinner on this side.

Two plates in one

Reversible Plate

Reversible plates are made from high-quality real plastic. Use one side for breakfast, but then, rather than wash, dry, rinse, and repeat, simply push on the middle of the plate. You'll hear a satisfying "pop" and, suddenly, the top is the bottom, the bottom is the top, and you're good to go for the next meal.

Flip the dirty plate...

...over. Press with thumbs until plate...

...pops through.

POP!

After breakfast, reverse the plate by popping the middle. The clean bottom now becomes the clean top. Lunchtime!

In case of ax-cidents

Band-Aid-Equipped Ax

Nothing brings on the tears quite like a boo-boo from a mishandled ax, and that's why we've taken the traditional ax design and added an important new feature: a hidden compartment in the handle that contains up to 24 Band-Aids.

Hidden compartment swings out of handle.

Works best with wooden shoes

The Xylaladder

Here's a way to change light-bulbs in the key of G. Each rung on the Xylaladder is manufactured and mounted to play a single note. Beginners can scale this unique stepladder from the bottom rung to the top to practice *do, re, mi,* while more advanced players will learn how to hop from rung to rung to play familiar tunes.

STEP-BY-STEP SONGS:

Up On the Roof

Stairway to Heaven

Stop fishing around in your pockets

Pocketless Velcro Pants

Groping around in pockets for stuff you can't see and don't even know if it's there is a frustrating blind man's game. The solution? Pocketless Velcro pants, the ultimate in see-through attire. For best use, attach matching bits of Velcro to all the stuff you normally carry around — keys, wallet, etc. Then, stick 'em on your pants. A brilliant invention in this time of greater transparency.

Rearview relief

Rearview Mirror–
Equipped Neck Brace

A nyone who's ever walked around with a stiff neck will appreciate the sheer relief built into this design. Two heavy-duty truck mirrors screw on to both sides of a standard neck brace. Result? No more blind spots. No more surprises from the rear.

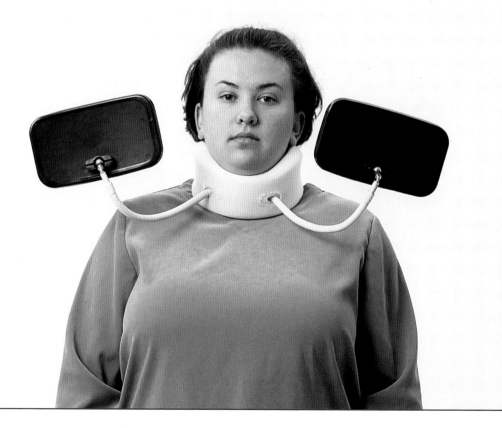

Puts wasted play energy to work

Lawnmowing Tricycle

Sure you love to watch your kid having fun outside, but wouldn't you love it even more if he were learning some important lawn-care basics at the same time?

Of course you would. And with this three-wheeling lawnmower, that's exactly what he'll be doing. This tricycle comes equipped with a push-style set of lawnmower blades between the wheels. Your kid will love the extra challenge and hey! He's out there pedaling around anyway! A win-win.

Give piece a chance

Pizza Spinner

Nothing's worse than the awkward moment that comes when you and your three or four co-pizza-eaters are staring at the last piece. No one's talking, but the tension's thick enough to cut with a pizza slicer.

Fortunately, we have a simple fix.

A center-mounted spinning arrow that will bring a little game show energy to that last-piece moment. Instead of the furtive grab and all the resentment and bitterness that inevitably follow, just hit the spinning arrow and let sheer dumb luck pick the eater.

Takes the frustration out of golf

Golf Club/Hole Digger

The bottom of this golf club is your basic ordinary golf club, but the handle is where the magic happens. It's actually a miniature posthole digger. Turn the club over, plunge it into the earth, and when you pull it out, you'll leave a perfect, regulation-sized golf hole.

Top end of club is a hole digger.

Now, instead of trying to hit the ball closer to the hole, you can move the hole closer to the ball! How's that for rethinking an old problem! (And by the way, if any of your fellow golfers are "sticklers" for the rules and try to say something, tell them to can it. We've done the research, there's no rule about moving holes.)

Make the new hole near the ball.

Dig hole.

Finish putt.

Puts the sound into pound

Whistling Sledge

Anyone who's ever built a railway or worked on a road gang knows that swinging a sledge all day in the hot sun can get to be tedious. That's why we've gone back to the drawing board and come up with a radical new sledgehammer design — one that takes the "hard" out of "hard labor."

How'd we do it? What's our secret?

Aerodynamically designed whistles. Each of our sledges comes equipped with four colorful plastic whistles attached to the forged steel head of the sledge. As you swing the hammer through the air, the four whistles automatically emit a cheerful, high-pitched whine. The result is a festive party feeling brought to the old chore of crushing rocks.

Cord Comb

The cord comb is a handy device for dealing with one of life's little headaches. Use it to pull the tangles out of tangled-up electric cords.

Leave a lasting impression

The Rubber Stampshake

Each rubber Stampshake is unique and embossed with the graphics of your business card or personal contact information. Using the sturdy elastic strap, wear it on your palm and keep it inked up. That's it. The rest is automatic. With a Stampshake on, every one of your handshakes leaves a permanently inked version of your business card. A salesman's dream.

Your hand

Your customer's

Why should hamsters have all the fun?
Automatic Dog Walker

Dog walking doesn't have to be unproductive down time. With this invention — a dual-tasker's dream machine — you can walk the dog at the same time as you watch TV or take a nap. The spinning wheel lets Biscuitbreath get his exercise while you hit the couch and grab a cold soda. A boon for anyone struggling to find enough time in the day to "do it all."

Conserves water

Salad Washer Showerhead

This is one of those "Why didn't I think of that?" ideas! A showerhead that doubles as a salad washer. These days in particular — when we're all doing everything we can to conserve resources — this is a gizmo that works for you AND the planet.

The salad washer screws on like an ordinary showerhead and shoots water out like an ordinary showerhead — but that's where the similarity stops. Turn it off, flip open the handy door, and you'll find all kinds of room for lettuce, cut vegetables, fruit, or even small dirty dishes. Fill it up, close the lid, take a shower.

After you've toweled off, just dump the vegetables into a bowl and take them out to the kitchen for chopping!

Make every day trash day!

Magical Disappearing Trash Bags

Taking the trash out just got a whole lot simpler. Use these specially printed "Property of U.S. Mint" trash bags and leave your garbage on the porch any night you like. In the morning they'll be gone. It's amazing!

Get those little suckers for good!

Bug Zapper Earrings

Pest control and fashion come together in these attractive battery-powered bug zapper earrings. Perfect for those sleeveless summer evenings when the little suckers are out there in force. Removable bottom tray makes it easy to clear out their toasted little carcasses when you get home.

Don't wash 'em! Melt 'em!

Ice Plates

All ice plate and silverware.

Have you ever stood in front of a sinkful of dirty dishes and just wanted to close your eyes while the whole problem just… sort of… went away?

Welcome to your dream come true. When your plates and silverware are made of ice, all you need to do is turn on the hot water.

To create this miracle, use this specially designed ice cube tray, fill it with water, and stick it in the freezer. An hour later, pull it out, pop out the plates and silverware, and serve dinner. Soon.

The mold

Kiss toilet seat cooties good-bye

The Multi-Seat Family Model

It's hard to talk about good family hygiene these days without talking about toilet seat cooties at the same time. They're there. We all know it. Squirming around in their disgusting little microscopic ways. A big yuck. But what can you do about them?

Meet the multi-seat family model. A "concept commode" for the modern health-conscious family. Pictured here is the standard four-seater (Mom, Dad, Junior, and a guest). But there's no reason the concept couldn't be extended, so to speak, up to 5, 6, even 7 seats. Sure you might need a little stepladder, but that's a small price to pay for the confidence of knowing that your seat was the only seat that your seat ever touched.

Rests weary chewing muscles

The Automatic Chew Machine

Here's a smart labor-saving device designed to deal with the simple fact that it's really boring to move your jaw up and down, up and down, up and down. The automatic chew machine is simple to operate (put food in mouth, place chin on cradle, switch on) and works off regular household current. A speed control allows you to pick up the pace when you only have time to eat and run.

*Like a sandwich
Bluetooth*

Hands-Free Sandwich Holder

Let's you work right through your lunch break!

If you live in the fast track (and who doesn't these days?) you'll appreciate the multi-taskability built into this invention. Instead of bringing your life to a screeching halt every time you have a ham sandwich, this adjustable neck-mounted, mouth-ready device allows you to keep right on texting, e-mailing, or channel surfing while you eat a handy sandwich.

*Gives tired
ears a break*

Stick-On Suction Cup Glasses

We broke the arms off a conventional pair of glasses and replaced them with one vacuum-powered, forehead-mounting suction cup. The result? The Glasses of the Future. Thanks to their unique design, suction cup glasses do not hang heavily on the ears nor do their little hinges break or arms snap at just the wrong irritating moment. Particularly great for pillow-based reading.

Ballcap Visor Caddy

Convenience, convenience, convenience. When it comes to personal organizational tools, it's hard to say the key rule too often. This experimental concept cap, for example, puts all of your daily essentials right where you can see and retrieve them instantly. No groping around in dark pockets.

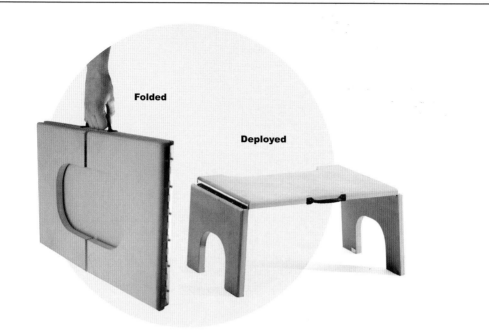

Folded

Deployed

You'll always have a seat when you bring it with you...

Subway Bunk Seat

This invention is all about comfort and convenience. With a subway bunk seat, you'll never have to stand in the aisle again. If your car or bus is full, just fold down the sturdy legs, fit them over the lap of the guy who probably shouldn't even be sitting in your seat anyway, and plop right down. It's quick. It's comfortable. And it's always there.

Dog food on demand
The KibbleBack

Here's a smart idea for active dogs that need constant "in-flight" refueling. The KibbleBack straps to your dog's back and, thanks to the mouth-mounted resupply pipe, Fido can stay fed and friendly all day long.

Prevents "rumper bumper"

Turn Signal Earrings

Tailgaters are an unfortunate fact of life: People who walk so close behind you it's annoying. But at least with turn signal earrings, you can eliminate one of the big issues, i.e., the personal rear-ender. Or, as some people call it, the "rumper bumper."

Here's how it works: As you prepare to turn, simply press the button on the handheld controller and the blinking light will give your tailgater a chance to slow down and yield.

Never lose your car
in the parking lot again

Flip-Up Car Sign

A low-tech solution to an enormous modern problem. This high-gloss sign mounts on sturdy hardware on top of your car. When you're driving, it folds down flat. When you park — say in the middle of some 40-acre, 6 million car lot — just lift it up and lock it down. With its bright, eye-catching graphics, you'll be able to see it from anywhere in the lot. So instead of wandering aimlessly around, you'll be able to look up and see your car, like an old friend, calling to you.

Over Here Idiot

Ever wonder what fruitcakes are good for?

Fruitcake Dumbbells

This custom-shaped, rubber-coated grip connects two fruitcakes to make a perfect 10-pound weight cake. Lasts for years.

Dog Return Collar

Here's a simple solution to the problem of wandering pets and worrying owners. These postage-paid, preaddressed collars will bring your wayward weimaraner or straying schnoodle right back home by return mail. If someone finds your beloved Barney lost and adrift, all they have to do is pop him into any mailbox and let the USPO take him from there.

Wherever you go, your plan goes with you

Hat-Mounted To-Do List

My To-Do's

A sk any successful business leader or NFL coach and they'll all tell you the same thing: Winners don't wander. They never take their eye off the ball. They keep distractions on the sidelines; they keep the target in the crosshairs; they play it one down at a time; they keep their head in the game, nose to the grindstone, and back to the wall. It's that simple.

But *how* in this day of 24/7 media overload? How do you keep your goals in focus with all that noise off the field?

Easy. Meet the hat-mounted to-do list. It doesn't flip up. It doesn't go away. No matter where you run, no matter where you hide, your plan stays front and center.

The hat-mounted to-do list is made out of 100% clear see-through

plastic and mounts to the hat with sturdy attachment fixtures for handling quickly changing priorities. Wipe-off marker included.

Works like a heads-up display to keep your priorities in view.

ASK ME ABOUT

MY

HEMORRHOIDS

How to keep that seat next to you empty

Seat Saver Sign

When you sit down in an airplane, and the seat next to you is empty, but there are still lots of people to come on board, do you find yourself worrying? In particular, do you worry that some huge person is going to sit next to you and steal the armrest and squeeze the very breath of life clear out of you?

Here's how to stop worrying and start relaxing. As soon as you sit down, slip on one of these hemorrhoid seat saver signs, lean back, and close your eyes. When they close the door, you can open them. And if there is only one seat on the whole plane that is empty, it'll be the one next to you.

Put your digestive problems behind you… way behind you

Vent Pants

Does your digestive chemistry interfere too often with your social life? Are you losing friends and business contacts from the unfortunate outcome of gaseous internal reactions? Are you, in other words, a victim of irrepressible intestinal eruptions?

If the answer to any of these questions is a resounding, resonant "Yes!" then you need to stay right where you are and keep right on reading, because this is your page.

Vent pants are designed to provide an outlet for digestive emissions of all types, regardless of strength or toxicity. Constructed of neoprene ducting, and sealed gasket construction, vent pants are completely hazmat certified.

Apart from the fire and safety benefits, vent pants can be your ticket to social and business success. You'll receive more invitations to indoor events. You'll find yourself invited to join group conversations. You'll reenter the social mix with greater pride and confidence. And best of all, you can eat whatever you like… beans, milk, leafy vegetables, etc. With vent pants, you can finally put your digestive problems behind you.

Vent should go to other room or exterior space.

Turns bad breaks into good

The Metal Detector/ Crutch Combo

Here's the item for people who aren't willing to let a little broken limb keep them from sudden riches. Each of these specially built crutches comes complete with all the electronics and sensor plates of a beachcomber-quality metal detector. After you've busted an ankle, don't you think you're about due for a better break? What a perfect time to hit the beach and find that treasure you know is out there waiting for you. The metal detector/crutch combo is designed to keep you headed towards your rainbow, even if you have to hobble to get there.

Sneezing in style
Sleenex Cuffs

When you're dealing with a nasty cold and runny nose, and a big sneeze is coming on, you don't have time to hunt around for a box of Kleenex. Your needs are now. That's why Sleenex cuffs make so much sense. Each Sleenex cuff is a full-sized roll of tissue, designed to fit snugly around your wrist and stay right with you all day. It's an attractive accessory and a 50-foot-long runny nose rubber, all wrapped up in one.

50-foot Sleenex roll fits on wrist.

Finally put that gym machine to work

The Quitter's Convert-a-Kit

Are you the owner of one of those huge, fabulous, multi-function gym machines? With all the weights and springs and so forth? They are amazing devices, and you should be quite proud to have one. But like many, you probably find yourself occasionally puzzled by a nagging question: What's it good for?

Up to now, of course, the answer has been "pretty much nothing," which is why they make such common and beloved garage sale items. But with the invention of the Quitter's Convert-a-Kit, all that has changed.

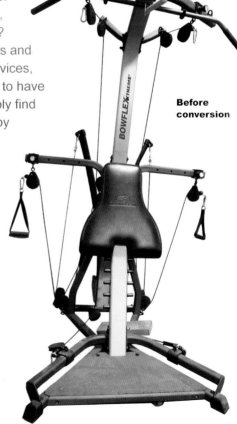

Before conversion

After conversion

The Quitter's Convert-a-Kit allows you to turn nearly every kind of exercise machine into a comfy television lounge chair complete with cup and snack holders. The kit comes with all the necessary hardware, instructions, and cushions. After just a few hours of easy assembly, you'll finally be able to haul your machine out of the attic or garage and down to the TV room where you'll be able to put it to good use at last!

*World's first comb
with a credit limit*

Credit Comb

Space is way too tight in today's crowded wallets for single-purpose anythings; that's why we added value and hair-care functionality to the standard credit card. With a dual-purpose credit comb, you can charge your purchases and still keep that well-groomed look, both at the same time.

A cell phone/shaver combo

The ScreenShaver

In all the hoopla about iPhones and all the amazing things they can do, one topic has never been properly addressed, and that is good facial grooming. Sure you've got fast Internet access, but you've also got a scuzzy 5 o'clock shadow and, for a lot of guys, that's what matters more, especially when it's Friday afternoon and they're looking at a hot date.

That's why we've created the ScreenShaver, an iPhone app that turns your smartphone into a smooth-shaving electric razor. Complete with three high-speed shaving heads, the ScreenShaver will give you the kind of close shave that only an Internet-enabled smartphone can deliver.

Three blades make for a smart shave.

Reduce your footprint

Eco-Friendly SnugFit Beach Towels

Unless you are shaped like a large rectangle, regular beach towels just don't fit very well. On top of that, regular beach towels waste valuable terry cloth and cover unnecessary beach. Compare that to SnugFit beach towels. SnugFit beach towels leave a smaller footprint and conserve resources while they boast a more flattering fit.

No more "corn tooth" surprises

Mirror Fork

How many times have you come back from a fancy dinner and discovered a monster corn goober stuck to your front tooth?

Embarrassing, isn't it? Well your solution is finally in your hand. Right on the other end of your fork, where you'll find a high-quality dental mirror that lets you inspect your teeth, in real time right between bites. Class up your act and clean up your teeth, right there at the table.

The scooter solution

Helmet- Mounted Rack

Convenience and comfort come together and sit right on top of your head in this simple scooter-friendly combo design. Put your books and lunch on the rack, hold them in place with the powerful spring, watch for low branches, and roll off to school.

Passing gas

Whoopee Ball

The whoopee ball is designed to inject a new air of excitement into football while giving fresh importance to the long pass and, of course, the tight end.

Thanks to its rugged construction, the ball is also the world's first NFL-endorsed whoopee cushion, designed to handle and throw as well as regulation — the difference comes in the catch (and, of course, the new fan favorite play, the fumble recovery).

Get your cushion cash back

Coin Return Couch

This concept couch comes equipped with a gravity-fed coin return system built under the cushions. Any out-of-pocket change falls into a hidden pipe that dumps it into the coin return mounted on the side of the couch.

Tip! When friends drop by, encourage them to sit on your couch and then turn them into profit centers by getting them to bounce around ("Check out the springs!"). After they leave, look to see what your take was.

Turns guests into profit centers.

Why blow when you can know?

Soup-Testing Spoon

Too Cold   Just Right   Too Hot!   Cooked Tongue!!

Never fear another bowl of hot soup again. With a thermometer-equipped soup-testing spoon, you will know before you blow.

Tired of waiting for people who won't pass the food?

Radio Control Serving Dish

othing is more frustrating when you're ready for seconds than getting people at the table to pass the peas (or pizza, or pie, or prunes, or…). But now, with the power of radio control technology in your hands, you can take a pass on frustration. Put the turkey on this remote control serving dish and then when you're ready, just push the button, steer around the salt, and roll that gobbler right back where it belongs.

Never stand in line again

The Belt Hook Hammock

Being stuck in an endless line just got a whole lot more relaxing. Simply hook the specially designed ends of this lightweight hammock onto the belts of the people who are in front and in back of you, kick back for a little snooze, and ask someone to wake you when you get to the front of the line.

Hands-free!
The Popcorn Headbucket

Get that tub of popcorn out of your hands and sit back to enjoy the movie. The popcorn headbucket fits snugly around your forehead and contains two full quarts of freshly buttered popcorn dispensed in a hands-free feeding trough. Comes complete with floss and handi-wipes.

The Sponge Bib Solution

Hey. Spit happens. So does spaghetti. And soup. And coffee. But with the sponge bib solution, you're ready. The sponge bib solution fits neatly around your neck and protects your tie, shirt, etc. from drips or slips. After the meal, remove, squeeze, rinse, and repeat.

Build a little buzz

Fly-Powered
Banner Ads

BUZZ's BBQ
1400 FECAL LANE

Are the flies in your house contributing in any way? Helping out? You're keeping food on the table, stocking the fridge, and what are they doing? Eating all they can get and putting their disgusting little feet on everything is probably the answer, right?

Right. So how would you like to change that? How would you like them to start "pulling their weight" for a change?

Meet "fly-powered banner ads." These handy little banners come attached to sticky pieces of thread. Put them on the windowsill and before you know it, your business message or social greeting is zooming around the neighborhood, getting the word out and spreading the message. Use them to announce a wedding or other special event. Use them to help find a lost cat. Or just use them to get your new business off the ground. The possibilities are endless.

Remember! In today's crowded market, it's all about the buzz.

You have bought your last piece of gum

NetGum

There's nothing quite as satisfying as a brand-new stick of gum. And nothing quite as sad as a flavorless wad of ABC ("already been chewed").

At least that's the way it used to be. But with NetGum, your mailman will take away your sadness and bring back the chewy good times. It's super simple. All you have to do is put your ABC gum in our postage-paid, preaddressed box and within 7 working days your gum will be returned to you completely recharged with a brand-new flavor. Build a queue of flavors from our list of zillions. And best of all? No late fees! Keep your old gum as long as you like.

NETGUM
1070 Refresh Way
Tall Tree, CA

Return your old gum for a new flavor.

Thigh-Mounted Cup Holder

Swivels when you stand up.

For everyone out there who'd like an extra shot of convenience with their coffee, this is the invention you've been waiting for. The thigh-mounted cup holder keeps your beverages either hot and handy or cold and convenient, all depending. And bonus! With its easy-rotate design, the thigh-mounted cup holder lets you sit or stand. Entirely up to you. Your drink is ready when you are.

Carbonate
your carrots

Flavorless Pop Rocks®

Flavorless Pop Rocks (no sugar, no calories, lots of zing) makes everything go snap, crackle, and pop. Once you've tried carbonated cauliflower, you'll never go back.

NET WT. 26 OZ. (1 LB. 10 OZ.) 737g

Socks-in-a-box?

Socks-by-the-Foot

Announcing a historic breakthrough in footwear technology. For the first time since mankind swung out of the trees, the human race now has the means to free itself from the tyranny of the missing sock. The solution ("socks-by-the-foot") works like this: A 100-foot-long single tube sock is wound into a box, much like a rope. Pull as much sock as you would like from the box, then cut it off and knot it. Presto! New matching sock!

ONE HUNDRED FEET INSIDE

Socks by the **Foot**

Don't take it camping

Helium Hide-a-Bed

Another lighter-than-air innovation. This is the world's first example of aero-furnishing, a cross between a blimp and a twin bed. By day, it goes where no bed has gone before: the ceiling.

By night, with the help of a handy pull-down cord, it comes down to earth (and sleeps like a cloud). The perfect sleep technology for people in tiny apartments.

Bonus for you guys out there: Because it's a true overhead bed, there's no need to make up the sheets and blankets since no one's going to see it up there anyway.

During day, bed
stores on ceiling.

Lawn care meets hair care

The Leaf Blower/ Hair Dryer

The leaf blower/hair dryer multi-unit is a stylish 5-horsepower hair care/farm implement that dries your hair to a soft, silken sheen at the same time as it blows those leaves to heck and gone.

Learn the color of your cat's neuroses

Mood Collars

Would you like to have a better understanding of your dog or cat? Where they're at emotionally? Mood collars — collars that change color depending on your pet's mood — can give you a window into the soul of your schnauzer, a peek into your Pekingese.

Displeased

Annoyed

Sullen

Privacy whenever you want it

Cell Foam Helmet

If you're like us, you're probably really irritated in restaurants and public areas when you have to take a call and the people around you don't clear out to give you a little privacy. What's up with that? We're wondering too, but the unfortunate truth is that people today are just not very considerate.

Fortunately, with a cell phone privacy helmet, you don't have to rely on the non-existent good manners of strangers. When an important call comes in, and you're out in public, just slip on this foam-insulated privacy helmet and yak away!

Fire
extinguisher

Whipped
cream

Is your kitchen a little storage-challenged?

Combo Cans

In those apartment kitchens where there's never enough shelf space, these handy combo spray cans are real lifesavers. Get the whole collection and "double" your storage space.

Whipping cream/fire extinguisher

Hairspray/Cheezy Whizzy

Primer coat/salad oil

Kick 'em 'n' stick 'em
Wall Walkers

Just because you've hit the wall is no reason to stop walking. With a pair of super-suction wall walkers, you'll discover your walls are made for walking.

Wall walkers are platform-based, slip-on, one-size-fits-all super-suction shoe enhancements. Designed to fit any shoe and equipped with industrial-grade suction cups, wall walkers aren't just perfect for window washers, they're perfect for anyone who's about ready to climb the walls. Just put your shoe onto the steel platform, twist the key to tighten the fit, and you're ready to kick 'em and stick 'em.

Prevents empty jar finger ick

The Double-Barreled Peanut Butter Jar

Plain good sense meets plain or crunchy. The visionary double-barreled jar design turns the bottom 2 inches of peanut butter into the top 2, like getting a brand-new jar just when the old one starts to get finger icky.

It's hard to say "brilliant" when you're talking about peanut butter jar design, but in this case, it's hard not to.

Fashion crashin'
Doll Jetpacks

Here's a great idea that lets everyone enjoy the fun of playing with dolls. Each jetpack comes with adjustable Velcro straps that can attach to any fashion doll in the house, even the kind in your little sister's room.

Once you've strapped the attractive fashionable jetpack on, slip her over the launch tube and STOMP on the booster pad! Blast off!

Stomp here.

Jetpack fits any fashion doll.

*Works best
at day games*

The Fanburn Hat

If you're serious about your team, here's a great way to show 'em where your love goes. The fanburn hat has your team's logo punched out of the back strap. Put the hat on, switch it around, and sit back while the sun does its UV thing (takes about an hour, depending). Afterwards, you can take your hat off and relax. With a fanburn on your forehead, nobody'll have any doubts about who they're dealing with.

It's all about safety

Beeping Backup Shoes

We started with a fashionable pair of formal shoes and looked to address one of the key issues for their wearers: back-up safety, especially for those living in houses with lots of dogs and small children.

We realized that ordinary shoes (pointy toes, rounded heels) are really only designed to go one way: forward. It's as if the original designers just pretended that people never walk backwards.

Of course they do, and that was the insight that drove this design. By adding GPS sensors, flashing back-up lights and a high-pitched warning "beep-beep," we created the first shoes that allow you to back up safely, confident that no one behind you will be caught unawares and run over or sat on.

Your own personal blast-off

Backpack Rocket

For 50 years scientists have been promising us jetpacks — individual rocket-powered backpacks so we can fly to work and the store, etc. And for 50 years all we've gotten have been lame excuses and crash landings. Finally — after all the false starts and broken promises — they're here. Designed by us. Cool working backpack rockets.

The secret?

We got back to basics. Instead of rocket fuel and flames, we went to compressed air and water. Starting with a converted 5-gallon water jug, we added a pressure valve and directional exhaust bell. Bold, simple, and powerful.

How does it work? Add 1 gallon of water. Fill with compressed air to just before the bottle blows up. Then locate yourself someplace where crashing won't hurt and crack the valve wide open. Blast off!

Oh yeah. Wear a helmet.

Fill bottle with a mix of water and compressed air.

121

Prevents having to tell the same story over and over

Story-Telling Slings

No plug, no battery

Wind-Powered Blender

Here's an environmentally sensitive blender that puts the clean power of the wind to work in your very own kitchen. This "green machine" needs no plug and no motor. Just mount it firmly to a counter or kitchen table using four heavy-duty anchor screws. Fire up a leaf blower (not included) and you're all set to mix, chop, grind, or blend.

Orange juice on the go

The Helmet Squeezer

Here's an invention that's all about just-in-time freshness: a specially designed helmet with an orange juice squeezer mounted directly to the top. Just mash down on an orange and the juice feeds directly through the in-mouth tube. Wear it anytime you need to combine cranium safety with tasty Florida refreshment.

Use it in class or in the backseat

The Travel BBQ

Nothing beats the taste of a home-grilled burger or rib, but when you're in class, at work, or on the road it's pretty hard to lug along the Weber.

At least it used to be.

The Travel BBQ is a cunningly designed 4-inch travel grill that weighs less than 8 ounces and packs neatly into your carry-on or backpack. Use it in class, in the backseat, or on the airplane tray table.

Just large enough for a single burger, buffalo wing, or small rib. Comes complete with one briquette.

Anti-Ant
Picnic Plates

These anti-ant plates are the perfect, yes, antidote to insects that come uninvited to your picnic meals. Each paper plate is attached to a 4-foot no-crawl-coated plastic stake. Drive the stakes into the ground at different heights, depending on the size of your picnicker.

**4-foot
no-crawl-coated
plastic stake**

The Very Lonely Person's Pillow

By adding two soft, plump, and friendly arms, we've created a true multi-purpose pillow, offering both head support and human companionship. Now anybody can have a shoulder to cuddle on and a hand to hold every night.

Turns closets into dining rooms

The Pull-Down Table Door

Here's a way to "discover" a dining table and room you didn't even know you had. The innovative pull-down table door works double duty. During the day, it's an ordinary closet door, but when the dinner bell rings, switch up the special hinges and presto/change-o! It pulls down for dinner.

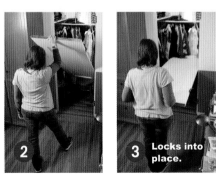

2

3 Locks into place.

1

Door pulls down.

Put some real spice in your life

Shaker Ring

Jewelry and condiments come together in a fashion accessory that blends style and savor. Wear these attractive shaker rings and everywhere you go you'll be a little spicier.

They did it, they can carry it

Dog Poop Pack

It's all about fairness. Like everybody else, dogs need to learn a little bit about responsibility. If you create the problem, you need to deal with the consequences. Is this such a hard concept to understand?

The Dog Poop Pack fits comfortably on your best friend's back and will carry up to two full bags easily. (And if he or she needs more than that, you have bigger issues.)

Puttin' the "hip"
back in the "whip"

Hula Whipper

By adding a squirt valve and cap to a specially modified food-grade hula hoop, we've turned an outdated fad into a handy kitchen tool. Just fill the hoop with heavy whipping cream, put the cap back on, and then shake it, shake it.

Fill.

Squirt.

Marshmallow Candle Cooker

Don't let the lack of a campfire stand between you and your marshmallow. This candle cooker is a handy portable alternative to messy smoky campfires. Simple to operate and easy to clean, the candle cooker goes anywhere. To the office, car, class… anywhere the taste of a freshly toasted marshmallow would really hit the spot.

Watch a movie while you clear a forest

Chainsaw DVD

Chainsaws might be fine for cutting firewood or clearing out brush, but they're not very entertaining.

At least they didn't used to be!

Introducing the world's first custom-modified saw, with a built-in DVD player entertainment system. Going out to cut trail will feel like going out to the drive-in. Pop in a new release, or maybe an old favorite, and catch a flick while you clear out a homestead.

You'll be hoppin' bad

Pogo X-Treme

Better put your seatbacks and tray tables in an upright position, because we've just put the "go" back with the "po."

Powered by a 12-horsepower 2-cycle scooter motor, this X-treme model is not your mama's 'stick. Designed for a new generation of thrill-seekers, this bad boy will clear a parked truck with more than 10 feet of daylight. You won't believe it 'til you hit the ground.

Stop bending over

Juggler's Retrieval Skirt

As anyone who's ever tried to learn how to juggle knows, there's a big problem with the force of gravity and step one is the same for every beginner. It's called "The Drop." (Step two, by the way, is called "The Bend-Over.")

At least it used to be. But with the juggler's retrieval skirt, you can take the bend-over right out of the lesson plan. With this invention, you'll be halfway to the Big Top while everyone else is still looking under the couch for their tennis balls.

Never needs washing

Underwaire Freshener

Be "washday-fresh" every day without ever doing the laundry. Each pair of these never-wash underwear comes complete with a snap-on pine-scented dangler. Recommended replacement period is 6 months, but it varies with the individual. (Ask your friends?)

Canstruction toy

Screw-Together Cans

hese precision-machined beverage cans screw together to make colorful and sturdy construction projects. No tools or extra parts required. A simple twist and the cans lock tightly together. You can make life-sized castles, bridges, robots… entire beverage villages. All you'll need is a little imagination and a steady supply of empties. (We'll let you solve that problem…)

Compatible with either diet or regular.

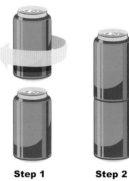

Step 1   **Step 2**

Empty cans screw together.

It's a green thing

Reusable Toilet Paper

Here's a resource-friendly solution to the wastefulness of disposable toilet paper. This endless roll of soft fabric lasts for a week of ordinary usage. Then, pop it in the laundry, roll it back up, and you're good to go all over again. In these times of diminishing natural resources, this is an idea that just plain makes sense.

Taming the pasta problem

The Spaghetti Organizational Plate

Italian food just got a whole lot more manageable. The spaghetti organizational plate puts a lid on the peril of pasta. Instead of fighting with a forkful of squirming noodles, suck them out one at a time through the center hole. No more mess. Perfect for when fancy guests are coming over and you want to make a lasting impression.

At least your mom will like it

Peez Dispenser

Here's the perfect pea-popping device that puts the fun back into the produce. The handy dispenser holds up to 20 garden-fresh peas. Lift the head on the monster and pop them into your mouth pea by automatic pea.

Culinary quick draw

Kitchen Tool Belt

Stop fumbling around in drawers for spoons and spatulas. When you're in the middle of meal preparation, you don't need distractions, you need ready-at-hand tools and condiments. This belt comes with all the standard utensils as well as quick-draw oil and vinegar.

Just pull up a chair

Reading Glasses

In the invention game, it's too often necessary to trade off form against function. It's tough to get both and creating something that looks as good as it works is a needle that most inventors can't thread.

But we're not most inventors. Proof? These pull-chain-equipped, battery-powered reading glasses. In one stroke, we've hit the trifecta of form, function, and fashion.

"Get outta my way!"
Outboard-Powered Floaty

This concept-floaty is a new combination of old ideas: one, the proven excitement of inflatable pool toys, and two, the fun of wind-in-your-face powerboating. Put the two together and the result is raw, in-your-pool thrills. The outboard is a 12-horsepower 2-cycle engine, while the floaty is a real hot-rod rubber ducky, designed and rigged for speed more than comfort.

A separately sold rope enables the craft to double as a water-skiing towboat.

Soil it 'n' toilet

Flush 'n' Wash Baskets

These handy plastic baskets fit snugly into any standard toilet and hold up to six pairs of socks, three boxers, and two shirts. Put into place (lift the seat first, guys!), add soap, and hit the lever two or three times. Afterwards, a couple more to rinse and you're good to go. It'll be the cleanest thing you've ever taken out of your toilet.

Fits all standard bowls.

Especially great for hotel travelers and apartment dwellers.

Solar
Cell

Self-powered

The Forever Flashlight

Here's an idea that just won't quit. The Forever Flashlight needs no battery and has no plug. It is powered by a high-performance solar cell that is located… directly in front of the flashlight, right in the beam. The beam powers the solar cell. The solar cell powers the beam. Which powers the solar cell. Which powers the beam. Which powers the solar cell. Which powers the beam… and so forth.

Any questions?

Spring loaded!
Zip-Back Zipper

Sometimes, it's the simplest ideas that have the most impact. Take, for example, this one — the automatic Zip-Back Zipper — a steel spring with one end attached to your zipper and the other to your pants. It's rustproof, reliable, and retractable. For anyone plagued with consistent half-mast issues, this could be the route to a whole new social acceptance.

Food Fight Plates

These weaponized plates are designed for use in school cafeterias where the possibility of hostilities is never far away. Note the use of deception in the design. Side A is your average plate; use it as you would any ordinary piece of dinnerware. Side B, on the other hand, is fitted with three secret springs designed to turn your average knife, fork, and spoon into food catapults. Load the catapults with food, hold the plate up like a shield, and one-by-one pull back on the spring-loaded silverware to launch an attack.

Spring-mounted silverware

Spring-loaded
Inside/ Outside Glasses

These spring-loaded reversible glasses combine the comfort of a headlock with the convenience of a combo optical unit. One side sunglasses; one side reading glasses. To go from one to the other, simply pull, switch, and snap back.

Outside

Inside

Two shoes in one

Reversible Shoes

Side A

Side B

Fashion and flexibility come together in these dual-purpose reversible shoes. During the day — at school or at work — wear them formal-side out. When the bell rings or the boss leaves, it's tennies time! Relax, put your feet up, and turn your shoes inside out.

Untie both front and back laces to turn inside out.

Save that parking spot!

The Inflato Hydrant

Imagine a parking spot. Permanently empty. Right in front of your home or office.

A dream?

Not anymore. With an inflatable hydrant in your purse or backpack, YOU will take control of your parking destiny.

Here is how it works:

On the day when you finally get your ideal spot, just pump up the inflatable hydrant and, when you leave, put it by your spot, a parking place "bookmark." Next morning, pull into the empty spot, deflate the hydrant, and put it in the trunk. That evening, when you leave, repeat the whole process. Simple, quick, and effective.

Free unlimited minutes for close friends

String Cell Phones

Here's an idea that will put a serious dent in your cell phone bill, especially if you spend a lot of time talking to close friends (30 feet is about the maximum). It consists of a string that attaches (via suction cups) to two cell phones. By pulling the string really tight, you can talk to your friend for free with unlimited minutes. No battery either, so it's a perfect "emergency phone," too.

Works up to 30 feet.

Rubber band–powered
Slingsocks™

You're looking at the world's first pair of dual-purpose, fully weaponized knitted footwear, designed for use in both peace and war. Absent hostilities, they act just like regular socks. But in the event of sudden attack, they turn into a powerful slingshot, able to repel attackers and launch deep into enemy territory.

A small belthook attached to the pouch allows the user to keep the slingsocks ready but at the same time safely out of the way. To use, simply sit down, roll back, load up, haul back, and let 'em have it.

Rest position   **Ready to fire**

Tasty Tee's

SnackShirts

Each of these T (for "tasty")-shirts holds delicious fruit, drinks, or snacks. Bananas, colas, ice cream… all fit neatly into their custom-designed pockets.

Ice cream pocket

Drink pocket

Turn up the volume
on your first impression

Video
Name
Tags

Video name tags are small LCD screens that display a short 10-second repeating loop of the wearer smiling, waving, and announcing his (or her) name. The powerful combination of video AND audio is a brilliant technological fix to the classic problem of meeting new people at a party or convention and making little or no impression. Trust us, if you wear a full-volume video name tag, that problem will be done.

HELLO

Never miss an inning again!

Sporta-Potty™

The bases are full but so is your bladder. And you're sitting in the middle of a long row full of big people holding lots of nachos and drinks.

Not a problem. At least not if you're sitting on a Sporta-Potty, the world's first true, fully featured, bathroom-equipped stadium seat.

The Sporta-Potty includes a soft cushion top, a handy cup holder, and most important of all, an internal, portable sealed-box "sanitary receptacle." Whenever you feel the need, flip up the top, expose the familiar seat, and you're good to go. Once your mission is accomplished, flip the seat back down and get right back to your game. With its unisex design, the Sporta-Potty works for both 🚺 and 🚹 .

World's first workout shovel

The ExerShovel

The ExerShovel is the world's first specially designed fitness shovel. We all know how shoveling ditches is a great cardio workout, but do you really want to tear up your yard while you're getting those pecs' and 'ceps?

Of course not. But with the ExerShovel, you can leave your yard alone. All you'll need is a little patch of dirt out behind your apartment and you can dig and dig for hours without going anywhere! How great is that?!

*Don't let a broken
leg keep you down*

Stilt
Crutches

Getting around with a broken limb doesn't
have to be the big drag that everyone
else always makes it out to be. Climb up on
these bad boys and you'll definitely get a
leg up on a high time. Specially designed to
accommodate broken legs, ankles, and feet,
as well as most reconstructive knee surgery.

Cuts feeding time in half

Twins Spoon

This handy double-barreled spoon is a boon for the harried mom of twins. Puts the efficiency back into feeding time. Two babies. One spoon. Genius.

Dead Bug Bingo

Here's a smart way to make the miles on those long family road trips fly by. Just stick this clear plastic bingo board to the inside of your windshield. As the bird doo and bugs hit your windshield, watch the excitement mount until that last splat and everybody hollers "bingo"!

It's a cap! It's a toothbrush! It's both!

SqueezyBrush

Another space-saving invention for the ounce-counting traveler. The SqueezyBrush replaces the cap on any standard toothbrush. Thanks to its specially machined interior (aka "hollow") you can squeeze the toothpaste through the brush and into the bristles. Perfect for one-handers, too (you pirates out there, take note).

Hollow. Squeeze to dispense.

Share smell lists

The Smell Pod

The smell pod is an invention that recognizes that people can smell as well as hear. The smell pod contains 5,000 distinct odors, ranging from burning leaves to wet dog, from grandma's attic to dentist's waiting room.

Naturally, everyone will have favorites, and so everyone will create personalized smell-lists, and then, depending on their mood, they'll choose one or the other. After a while, we will come out with smart smell pods too, so that you can download different smells and when your phone rings, it won't; it'll smell. (Of course, you can assign different smell tones, too. So different friends will smell different. Your sweetheart will be lavender; your boss can be postdigestive beans.)

Read my mind

The Thinking Person's Headband

For those times when you actually do want people to know what you're thinking, we've created this specially designed headband with attached whiteboard "thought balloons" and wipe-off marker included. Perfect for the kind of communication that can be hard to get out of your mouth, but still, it's something you want them to know.

"I don't remember your name."

Downy soft bookcovers

Pillow Book Jacket

Place head here.

This invention protects your valuable textbooks at the same time as it provides you a place to close your eyes and concentrate without distraction on what you've just read. It consists of a spandex book sleeve designed to fit most standard textbooks and sewn together with a pillowcase. Slip a small pillow in and protect your textbook against the shock of sudden drops at the same time as you turn your book into a comfortable quiet-time place.

Pillow

Overhead view

Scrub 'n' brush

Shower-Mounted Toothbrush

Multi-task in the shower with this handy wall-mounted toothbrush.

Flip-flops that don't flap

Snap-On Shoes

Here's a unique idea! Footwear that combines the comfort of slip-ons with the security of a rodent kill-trap.

We all know how comfortable they are, but the problem with slip-ons is… they slip off! To fix that problem, we borrowed an old trick from the days of the frontiersmen: spring-loaded leg traps.

Here's how flip-flop trapshoes work. Instead of a limp rubber strap, trapshoes have a spring-loaded wire bail. At night, haul the wire bail back and hook it into place onto the hair trigger. In the morning, hop out of bed and bingo! You're in! No more worrying about your shoes coming off at embarrassing moments during the day.

Bonus! If mice are a problem around the house, try setting up your shoes with a small piece of cheese.

Puts the fun back in traffic citations

Scratch-Off Parking Tickets

Finding a parking ticket under your windshield wiper can be an annoyance, a drop of rain on your sunny day. But it doesn't have to be. With this one simple innovation, that can all change in Vegas time.

Here is how it goes: Let's say you've just gotten a big fat parking ticket. You're saddened. Disappointed even. But then you look again. Your ticket is one of the new kind. You have options. You don't just have to take your lumps and pay up. You can scratch off the double-or-nothing window. If you're a winner, *you can toss it and walk!* Or maybe you want to take a shot at the grand prize? At 10-1 odds against, the city will owe YOU the fine.

Feeling lucky?

PARKING CITATION

EITHER PAY UP — OR — TAKE A CHANCE!!!

LICENSE PLATE NUMBER

PLATE TYPE
PAS OR ○ TRK ○ TXI
STATE

VEHICLE MAKE

VEHICLE IDENTIFICATION NUMBER

ISSUE DATE
MO   DAY   **20**
TIME OF VIOLATION

AT: STREET NO.

STREET NAME

ISSUED BY
SIGNATURE: **X**

☞ DOUBLE MY FINE! ☜
☞ ZERO FINE! ☜
☞ WE OWE **YOU** THE FINE!!

WHICH IS IT?
YOU WON'T KNOW
UNTIL YOU...

SCRATCH!

The hotter the day, the higher the price

Weather-Sensitive Vending Machine

If you think about it, vending machines aren't much more than big dumb refrigerators that won't let you in unless you pay them. In that way, they're like selfish bullies. But where does it say they can't be more? Much more! It's just a question of better design.

Take for example this design, the weather-sensitive vending machine. It "thinks" about what it's charging. On really hot days, it raises the cost of its drinks; on cooler days, it drops it. Scientists call this "artificial intelligence." You or I would call it "being a real jerk." But whatever you call it, there's no doubt it's a clever innovation that does a good job of turning a dumb machine into a thinking human. An evil thinking human, of course, but still…

Environmentally friendly

Rubber Band–Powered Saw

Put the power of the rubber band to work for you. This saw of the future is quiet, efficient, and best of all? No plug. Use it when the cord won't reach or when the kids are still asleep. Saves money, too! Requires two XXXL rubber bands.

Insta-wig-out
The Hairy Hoody

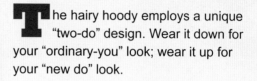

The hairy hoody employs a unique "two-do" design. Wear it down for your "ordinary-you" look; wear it up for your "new do" look.

Finish that nap

Snooze-Equipped Smoke Alarm

Everyone knows how loud and annoying today's smoke alarms are, how disruptive they can be when you're on the phone or even when you're just trying to relax. It's a problem. But rather than curse the darkness, we decided to light a candle.

We took the standard smoke alarm design and added a key ("why-didn't-they-think-of-this-before?") feature: a snooze button. Now if the alarm goes off you can still finish your call or nap without having to deal with a lot of disruption.

Haven't we met before?

The Perfect Date

Here's an idea that will enable you to sit down with an attractive, intelligent, witty, and well-mannered dinner companion every night. You!

This portable mirror sets up easily on any table directly in front of you. After having a lovely meal with yourself, fold it neatly away, and thanks to the handy handle, the two of you can go home together.

*Feel better
about saying "yes"*

Ballcap
Backscratcher

Be a self-sufficient back scratcher, the master of your own massage. Simply nod your head up and down, and suddenly the world seems like a better place.

Make up your bed and pick up your room in one second

The Pull-Down Perfect Bedroom

1 Pull down photo.

The difference between a neat and tidy bedroom and a messy one really has to do with nothing more than its appearance. And appearances, of course, can be deceiving. When you add to that the fact that true beauty lies below the surfaces, then it becomes doubly surprising when you realize how many parents are hung up on the surface appearance of bedrooms.

But here's an invention that can help, if your parents are misled in this way.

It's a photograph of a perfect bedroom printed on a pull-down shade that can be mounted in the doorway. Regardless of what your room really is, you can pull down this picture and fix its appearance in an instant.

Is this cheating? A true philosopher would say absolutely not. You're "fixing" the appearance of the room, right? And since the appearance was the problem in the first place, you're good. (Don't you love philosophy?)

② Room looks better…

③ …instantly.

Draw your own bowls and plates

The 50-Foot Paper Plate

50 feet of paper mounts to end of table.

Take the convenience of paper plates and multiply it by 50. This super-long paper plate mounts on a roller on the end of the table. Pull out enough to cover the table for every meal. Then make everyone use markers to draw personal eating zones, larger or smaller depending on appetite. After the meal, just rip off the whole thing and toss it! No muss, no fuss!

If you're hungry, draw a big plate.

There's no rule about having to draw round plates.

*Dental care when you
need it the most*

The LolliBrush

The LolliBrush is the world's first dentist-friendly stick-mounted confectionery, designed to put dental hygiene into your mouth right when you need it the most.

The moment you finish this yummy lollipop (14 different flavors) you'll discover that a toothbrush is already in your mouth! How about that for perfect timing?

What happens down there, stays down there

Soundproof Underwear

If your digestive process leads to the occasional embarrassing noise, then this could be an important innovation for you. What is it? Underpants that have been manufactured out of acoustic foam, a material specially designed to deaden sound.

Since it's made entirely from foam, soundproof underwear is obviously warm and comfortable, but its real virtue lies in its ability to kill uninvited noises. It knows (in other words) how to keep a secret.

Prescription sushi
Chopglasses

Chopglasses is an idea conceived at the (recently discovered) crossroads of European eyewear and Asian silverwear. On one end, stylish reading spectacles; on the other, easy-to-use bamboo chopsticks. Works as well for sushi as it does for small print.

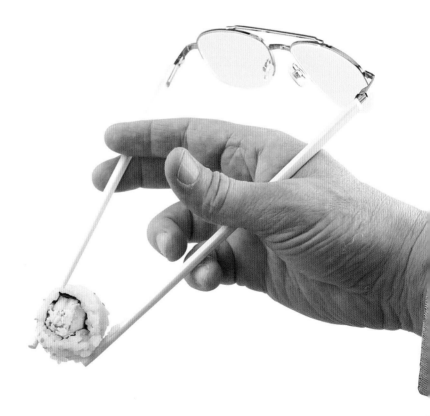

The Human Roller Bag

This is an energy-saving two-part invention: coaster shoes on the feet, and an extend-a-handle frame on the back. Put on the shoes, get some sturdy person to grab the handle, lean back, and away you go.

And we own the patent!

Never-Ending Ball-Drop Machine

Here's a simple solution to that pesky global warming problem. This machine runs using the never-ending power of the magnet and gravity. No coal, no oil, no nothing. Shown here is the mini-demonstration model. But obviously the idea could be scaled up with larger magnets and balls to the point where cities could build enormous banks of these machines and use them to run power generators. Clean and resource-friendly, this little machine is a game-changer.

Let's just get it out there…

The Truth Belt

Honesty. That's what we're all about. We don't like secrets; we don't like guessing games. Just like you, gentle reader, we welcome the fresh air and sunlight of openness and full disclosure.

That's why we have designed The Truth Belt. An attractive accessory that tells the world that here stands an honest man. Or woman.

*In recognition of the fact that the real truth can be complicated and often demands a degree of flexibility, The Truth Belt comes with a discreet 4 inches of spandex in the back.

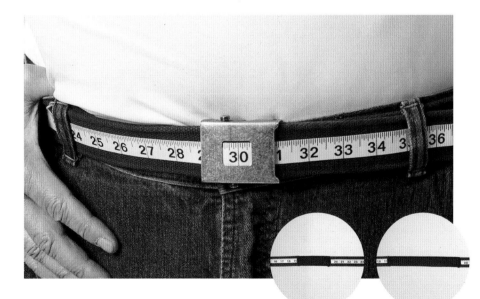

**Spandex allows you to stretch
the truth if necessary.**

Bring your own breeze

Sail Wagon

Here's the perfect way to set sail without going anywhere near the water. This innovative sail wagon design comes equipped with a 4-horsepower leaf blower mounted to the back.

All you need to do is hoist the sail, fire up the leaf blower, and you'll have a stiff breeze on your stern no matter the weather. Use the handle to chart your course and you'll be the captain of your own craft, master of your own destiny. Pack a lunch, weigh anchor, and cast your fate to (your own) wind.

A never-ending contest

We're Saving This Page for Your Idea

Send us your invention.

We've seen *our* inventions, now we want to see yours.

Come up with your own invention, draw a little sketch of it and drop it in the mail to us. If it has that special blend of brilliance and deep dumbery that we seem to like so much, we'll include it in a future printing of this book, on the blank page that we've saved for you.

Klutz/Weird Inventions
450 Lambert Ave.
Palo Alto, CA 94306

Draw your invention and describe it, and drop it in the mailbox.

Deadline? What deadline? Our contests are never-ending. We'll just name new winners and switch inventions every time we reprint the book.

Our lawyer wants you to know: If your idea is really practical and will make you a million dollars, don't send it to us. Keep it and make your million. And then send us half since we were the ones who gave you the assignment. Any inventions that come to us go into a big public mix, so if you want them kept as your property or secret, please don't send them in since they won't be after you do. By mailing them in, you are giving us permission to reprint them in future editions of this book where everyone else will see them and probably make lots of money from them. Except not you.

Our lawyer

Thanks, by the way.

How We Did This Book

The 162 inventions described in this book came to these pages through many different doors. A few of them are old patents, at least one is a still-active patent, a couple of others are the brainchildren of contraptioneers (especially Rube Goldberg, Kenji Kawakami, André Montejorge, and Phillip Garner), but the vast majority came out of the bad dreams, brainstormers, and collaboration between designers, editors, and inventors at Klutz and IDEO Toy Lab.

The brainstorming process we used is one that IDEO Toy Lab has refined and perfected over the years and it's one that actually has a firm(ish) structure, even though the outcomes are reliably unpredictable. A table is filled with people. Sugar, in some form, is provided. The rules to the game are painted on the wall.

The Rules to an IDEO Brainstormer	The Ingredients
1 Defer judgment.	
2 Go for quantity.	
3 Encourage wild ideas.	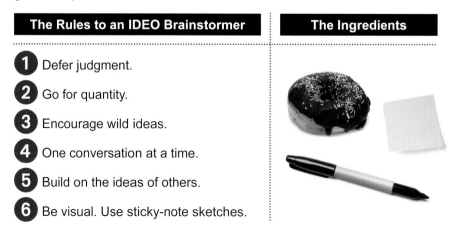
4 One conversation at a time.	
5 Build on the ideas of others.	
6 Be visual. Use sticky-note sketches.	

A challenge is written on the wall. It might be specific ("Blend two things. One, you bought at Home Depot. The other, at a gag shop"). Or, it might be more general ("Come up with a list of things that bug you in everyday life").

Sharpies® and sticky notes are everywhere on the table and, for 5 minutes exactly, everyone fills sticky notes with single ideas ("A welcome mat crossed with a whoopee cushion" or "People try to make me eat vegetables"). At the 5-minute mark, everyone puts down their Sharpies and eats more sugar before starting another 5-minute clock and another pile of sticky notes is filled with the "mutts" that came out of the Home Depot/gag shop matches, or solutions to the daily problems. In this way, you get a welcome mat that makes a farting noise or a picture of a clean plate you put over your vegetables.

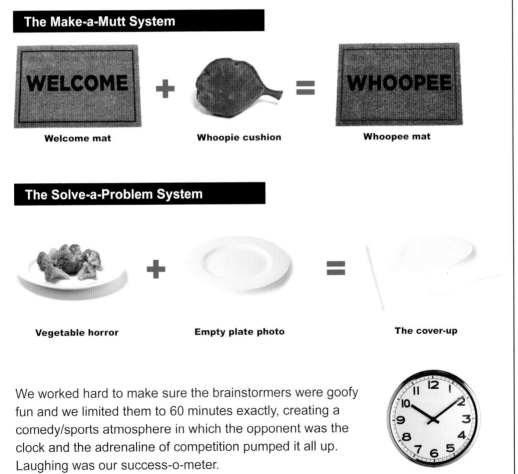

The Make-a-Mutt System

WELCOME + = WHOOPEE

| Welcome mat | Whoopie cushion | Whoopee mat |

The Solve-a-Problem System

+ =

| Vegetable horror | Empty plate photo | The cover-up |

We worked hard to make sure the brainstormers were goofy fun and we limited them to 60 minutes exactly, creating a comedy/sports atmosphere in which the opponent was the clock and the adrenaline of competition pumped it all up. Laughing was our success-o-meter.

The opponent

Last Step: The Group Build

The final step in the brainstorming process is the most important: the group build. Call it the "make it better" machine: One idea goes into the front end, a better idea comes out the back end.

Here's how it should go. Everyone presents their sticky notes to the group and puts them on the wall. Each of them is universally beloved since every idea is a point scored against the other team (the big bad clock).

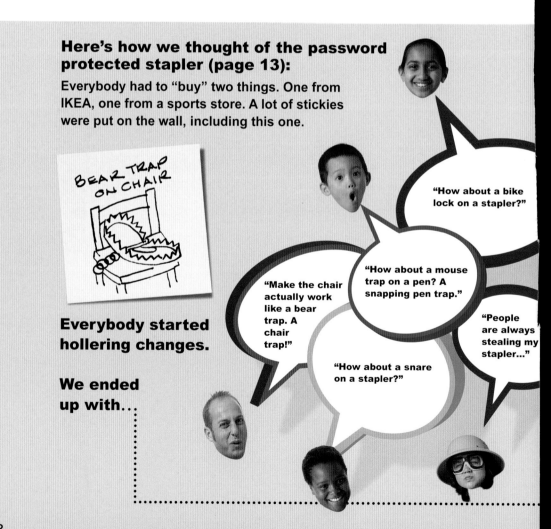

Here's how we thought of the password protected stapler (page 13):

Everybody had to "buy" two things. One from IKEA, one from a sports store. A lot of stickies were put on the wall, including this one.

BEAR TRAP ON CHAIR

Everybody started hollering changes.

We ended up with...

"How about a bike lock on a stapler?"

"Make the chair actually work like a bear trap. A chair trap!"

"How about a mouse trap on a pen? A snapping pen trap."

"People are always stealing my stapler..."

"How about a snare on a stapler?"

Often the sticky notes become the launching pad for further group discussion (the all-important "build"). This step — the most important one — goes a lot like a game of charades. Everybody hollers out random ideas, pushing the original idea in different directions. Nobody EVER says anything negative about any idea. The goal was always quantity ("We need MORE!") and the quality, remarkably, took care of itself. We threw a lot of balls up and some of them, inevitably, went in. Here for example, is how the group turned a bear trap on a chair into a password protected stapler.

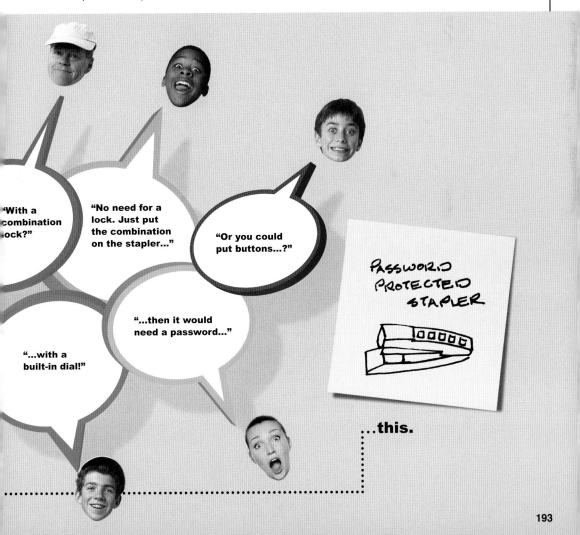

www.klutz.com
www.ideo.com

Who Did This Book

THE KLUTZ BOOK OF INVENTIONS is the result of a year-long collaboration between Klutz and IDEO, the legendary design and innovation firm. The Klutz team was led by John Cassidy and the IDEO Toy Lab team by Brendan Boyle.

Much of the collaboration took place in the form of brainstorming over lunch hours at the IDEO Toy Lab. Fueled by life-threatening dosages of pizza and doughnuts, zillions of ideas were fomented and eventually whittled down and refined into the 162 winners that you see here. The "invention-making" process that we used is based on one that IDEO developed, which we just described.

Both Klutz and IDEO Toy Lab are based in Palo Alto, CA, and share a firm belief in the powers of design and innovation and prototyping. And funny stuff.

Key members of the Klutz braintrust were David Avidor, Michael Sherman, Nicholas Berger, and Eleanor Hanson. Key members of the IDEO team were David Webster, Brian Witlin, Peter McDonald, Carly Geehr, Michelle Lee, and Miguel Cabra. Most of the ideas in this book were actually built in the IDEO prototype shop by Nathan Whipple and then photographed in action. An exhibition of them is in the planning stages and for more information about that, or anything else about Klutz or IDEO Toy Lab, please check out our websites.

Chief Inventioneers
John Cassidy
Brendan Boyle

Design
Kevin Plottner

Photography
Peter Fox
John Cassidy

Editorial Assistance
Rebekah Lovato

Production
Gary Mcdonald
Mimi Oey

Prototypes
Nathan Whipple
Joe Wilcox
Eleanor Hanson
Laura Torres
Charlotte Hutter-Brock

Acknowledgments & Inspiration
Philip Garner
Rube Goldberg
Kenji Kawakami
Annie Kutzscher
André Montejorge
Michael K. Proctor
Aya Tsukioka
University of Art and Design, Lausanne

Help/Contributors
David Avidor
Nicholas Berger
Michael Sherman
Will Abbott
Edith Barr
Dennis Boyle
Peter Bronk
Greg Brown
Tim Brown
Miguel Cabra
Paul Chaiken
April Chorba
Jim Collins
Brian Cook
Alex Coriano
Vicki Dalrymple
Andy Deakin
Kyle Doerksen
Elysa Fenenbock

Jim Feuhrer
Jessica Foley
Susan Fox
Carly Geehr
Adam Glazier
Derek Goodwin
Hans-Christoph Haenlein
Eleanor Hanson
Gerry Harris
Bladen Hawthornthwaite
Joani Ichiki
Anne Johnson
David Kelley
Tom Kelley
Vlasta Komorous-King
Kara Krumpe
Lauren Kutzscher
Michelle Lee
Gus Liu
Brian Mason
Peter McDonald
Nacho Mendez
Jaclyn Nolan
Woo Jin Park
Karen Phillips
Kevin Plottner
Mike Pollock
John Ravitch
Maria Redin
Dan Roddick
Diego Rodridguez
Jesse Silver
Mary Simon
Adam Skaates
Rochael Soper
Neil Stevenson
John Stoddard
David Strong
Joerg Student
Linden Tibbets
Dorinda von Stroheim
David Webster
Erik Welker
Nathan Whipple
Joe Wilcox
Brian Witlin
Alison Wong

Models
Doug Analla, Kelly Ariagno, Ashvin Ashoke, Andre Augustin Jr., David Avidor, Armin Bautista, Nicholas Berger, Ruchi Bhandari, Camden Boyle, Scott Bryan, Buzzy the Fly, Nancy Cassidy, Scott Cassidy, Gary Champagne, Marcel Colchen, Cindy David, Susan DeLance, Deja Delaney, Kyle Doerksen, Dean Donat, Mitch Donat, Dewitt Durham, Avery Field, Bo Field, Daisy Fleming , Kaela Fox, Susan Fox, Framz, BJ Garvey, Sophia Hackworth, Zara Kestrel Harwell, Caleb Hauser, Bart Heichman, Brynna Heichman, Carrie Heichman, Cole Heichman, Nathan Heichman, Gary Hinze , Hipper, Yoshka Hoelzle, Nina Hunt, Amy Jennison, Anushka Joshi, Joseph Kadifa, Jim Kelly, Carolyn Kramer, Dick Kramer, Ollie Kutzscher, Debra Lande, Amanda Levinson, Louie the Bulldog, Rebekah Lovato, Jaime Martinez, Gary McDonald, Colin Mills, Eric Mills, Mitchell, Eden Rose Murray, Christian Oey, Bill Olson, Greg Osborne, Leo Rose-Levin, Sal Rose-Levin, Pablo the Magnificent, Reid Price, Devon Proctor, Adam Rosenblatt, Ben Saenz, Jeremy Samos, Schnoo, Michael Sherman, Adam Skaate, Emmett Stanley, John Stirrat, Chipper Stotz, Joe Street, Maisey or Anna Street, Jasmine Tantivilaisin, Kyle Talbert, Cass Taylor, Linden Tibbets, Rick Tipton, Jill Turney, Sergio Valente, David Webster, Joe Wilcox, Stephanie Wong, Erik Young, Lou Young, and the staff at Cody Anderson Wasney Architects

Art Credits

Page 1: Bowling ball © iStockphoto.com/NickyBlade. Page 6: Lightbulb © iStockphoto.com/ElementalImaging; Wheel © Dmitry - Fotolia.com. Page 8: DVD player © Pedro Díaz - Fotolia.com. Page 19: Pacifier © iStockphoto.com/Laborer; Dog © iStockphoto.com/edfuentesg; Pacifier in mouth © nik0s - Fotolia.com. Page 23: Parking lot © iStockphoto.com/Sparky2000. Page 27: bathtub © iStockphoto.com/seanfboggs. Page 33: Toilet paper holder © iStockphoto.com/kingvald. Page 38: Hanger © iStockphoto.com/skodonnell. Page 39: Bike seat © iStockphoto.com/SilviaJansen. Page 48: Toilet paper dispenser © iStockphoto.com/ugurhan. Page 53: Placemat © iStockphoto.com/claylib. Page 62: Music notes © iStockphoto.com/linearcurves. Page 70: Background © iStockphoto.com/jfelton. Page 78: Woman © iStockphoto.com/Deklofenak; Traffic lights © iStockphoto.com/svengine. Page 80: Dumbell © iStockphoto.com/bluestocking. Page 81: Mailman © Comstock Images (RF)/Getty Images. Page 89: Frame © iStockphoto.com/redmal. Page 107: Tape measure illustration © iStockphoto.com/piccerella. Page 108: Air tank © iStockphoto.com/tap10. Page 111: Cat © Imagentix/Alamy. Page 116: Jar © iStockphoto.com/winterling. Page 119: Shoes © iStockphoto.com/nico_blue; Alarm © iStockphoto.com/RonTech2000. Page 137: Underwear © iStockphoto.com/stuartbur. Page 138: Can illustrations © iStockphoto.com/groupera. Page 140: Toilet © iStockphoto.com/Creative. Page 145 & back cover:

Floaty photo © ILP/Swimline – Edgewood NY. Page 153: Fire hydrant © Marcia Cirillo; Air pump © chas53 - Fotolia.com. Page 154: Cell phones © iStockphoto.com/Matejay and © iStockphoto.com/macroworld. Page 158: Fans © Fotolia VI - Fotolia.com. Page 162: Windshield © iofoto - Fotolia.com. Page 169: Car illustration © iStockphoto.com/roccomontoya. Page 170: Thermometer © iStockphoto.com/step2626; Ice photo © iStockphoto.com/JanPietruszka. Page 183: Girl © iStockphoto.com/perkmeup; Business woman © iStockphoto.com/jhorrocks. Page 189: Lawyer © iStockphoto.com/fstop123. Page 190:

Doughnut © iStockphoto.com/ronen; Note © iStockphoto.com/bluestocking; Pen © iStockphoto.com/DNY59. Page 191: Whoopee cushion © iStockphoto.com/Joe_Potato; Welcome mat © iStockphoto.com/SAMIphoto; Broccoli © iStockphoto.com/LauriPatterson; Plate © iStockphoto.com/bluestocking; Clock © iStockphoto.com/Ridofranz. Page 193: Woman's face © Valua Vitaly - Fotolia.com. Page 197: Shoe © dim@dim - Fotolia.com; Bolt © Jiri Hera - Fotolia.com; Parachute © iStockphoto.com/SiriGronskar; Television © iStockphoto.com/ Palto.

Remoteless TV

The Entertainmop

The Outtakes

A great many things that we prepared for this book were cut as the editing process went on. Here are a few.

Combination Nose Hair Trimmer/BBQ Igniter

Swiss Army Broom/ Mop/Rake

Kitty Glitter

StayDry Surfboard

LED Bumper Stickers

Rubber Foot Dip

Powered Cotton Swab

Pepper grinder/ Baseball bat combo

High-Heel Skates

Edible Chopsticks

Battery Charger Powered by Hamster Wheel

Parent/Teacher Secret Hypnotism Ring

Mosquito Attractant Spray (use on friends)

Lawnmower/Baby Stroller Combo

Toilet Seat/Scale Combo

Adjustable High Heel

Onion Knife

Gag Shop Parachute

Other Books By the Same Klutz Guys Who Did This One

**Encyclopedia
of Immaturity:
Volume 1**

**Encyclopedia
of Immaturity:
Volume 2**

Animation

Tricky Video

KLUTZ

Free Mail Order Catalog Available

To request a free copy of our mail order catalog, go to klutz.com/catalog.

Become a Klutz Insider and get e-mail about new releases, special offers, contests, games, goofiness and who-knows-what-all. If you're a grown-up who wants to receive e-mail from Klutz, head to www.klutz.com/insider.

If you don't like computers, give us a call at 1-800-737-4123 (9–5 PST, M–F) or drop us a line at 450 Lambert Ave., Palo Alto, CA 94306.